PRAIRIE DOGS PERCHING: COUNTING BY 3s

by Amanda Doering Tourville

illustrated by Sharon Holm

Content Consultant: Paula J. Maida, PhD, and Terry Sinko, Instructional Support Teacher

VISIT US AT
WWW.ABDOPUBLISHING.COM

Published by Magic Wagon, a division of the ABDO Publishing Group, 8000 West 78th Street, Edina, Minnesota 55439.

Printed in the United States.

Text by Amanda Doering Tourville
Illustrations by Sharon Holm
Edited by Patricia Stockland
Interior layout and design by Becky Daum
Cover design by Becky Daum

Library of Congress Cataloging-in-Publication Data

Tourville, Amanda Doering, 1980–

 Prairie dogs perching : counting by 3s / by Amanda Doering Tourville ; illustrated by Sharon Holm.

  p. cm. — (Count the critters)

 ISBN 978-1-60270-266-0

 1. Counting—Juvenile literature. 2. Multiplication—Juvenile literature. 3. Prairie dogs—Juvenile literature. I. Holm, Sharon Lane, ill. II. Title.

 QA113.T687 2009

 513.2'11—dc22

2008001623

You can count faster when counting
by threes. Count by threes with a town
of prairie dogs on the wild prairies of
North America.

Three prairie dogs work on the wild prairie. They dig new tunnels to connect their burrows. Three prairie dogs live together in a town.

21 22 23 **24** 25 26 **27** 28 29 **30**   **0 + 3 = 3**

Six prairie dogs stand lookout on the wild prairie. They perch atop their burrow hills and look for danger. Count them slowly: one, two, three, four, five, six. Count them quickly by threes: three, six. Six prairie dogs live together in a town.

Nine prairie dogs keep their families safe on the wild prairie. They bark out a warning when danger is near.

Bark! Bark!

1 2 **3** 4 5 6 7 8 **9** 10 11 **12** 13 14 **15** 16 17 **18** 19 20

Count them quickly by threes:
three, six, nine. Nine prairie
dogs live together in a town.

Twelve prairie dogs run for their lives on the wild prairie. They dive into their burrows for safety. Count them quickly by threes: three, six, nine, twelve. Twelve prairie dogs live together in a town.

21 22 23 **24** 25 26 **27** 28 29 **30**   **9 + 3 = 12**

Fifteen prairie dogs peek out from their burrows on the wild prairie. They call to each other when it is safe to come out. Count them quickly by threes: three, six, nine, twelve, fifteen. Fifteen prairie dogs live together in a town.

1 2 **3** 4 5 **6** 7 8 **9** 10 11 **12** 13 14 **15** 16 17 **18** 19 20

21 22 23 **24** 25 26 **27** 28 29 **30**

12 + 3 = 15

Eighteen prairie dogs meet on the wild prairie. They welcome their family members by kissing them.

1 2 3 4 5 6 7 8 9 10 11 12 13 14 15 16 17 **18** 19 20

Count them quickly by threes: three, six, nine, twelve, fifteen, eighteen. Eighteen prairie dogs live together in a town.

15+3=**18**

Twenty-one prairie dogs feed on the wild prairie. They munch on grasses, roots, and seeds. Count them quickly by threes: three, six, nine, twelve, fifteen, eighteen, twenty-one. Twenty-one prairie dogs live together in a town.

1 2 **3** 4 5 **6** 7 8 **9** 10 11 **12** 13 14 **15** 16 17 **18** 19 20

21 22 23 **24** 25 26 **27** 28 29 **30**   18 + 3 = **21**

Twenty-four prairie dogs groom themselves on the wild prairie. They clean their fur to get rid of dirt and bugs. Count them quickly by threes: three, six, nine, twelve, fifteen, eighteen, twenty-one, twenty-four. Twenty-four prairie dogs live together in a town.

21 22 23 **24** 25 26 27 28 29 30   21+3= **24**

Twenty-seven mother prairie dogs get ready for their pups. They line their burrows with soft grass.

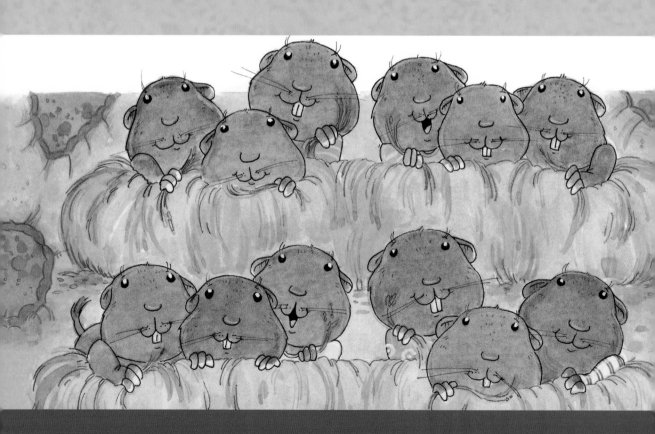

Count them quickly by threes: three, six, nine, twelve, fifteen, eighteen, twenty-one, twenty-four, twenty-seven. Twenty-seven prairie dogs live together in a town.

Thirty prairie dog pups are born on the wild prairie. Count them quickly by threes: three, six, nine, twelve, fifteen, eighteen, twenty-one, twenty-four, twenty-seven, thirty. Thirty prairie dog pups have joined the prairie dog town.

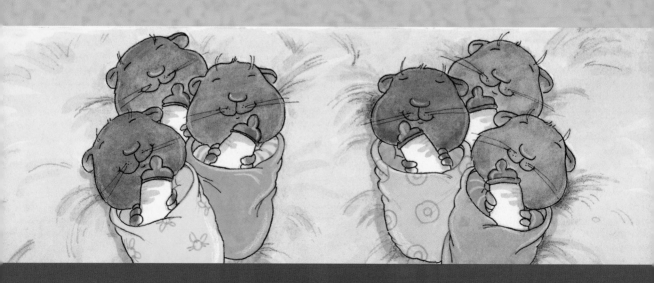

1 2 **3** 4 5 **6** 7 8 **9** 10 11 **12** 13 14 **15** 16 17 **18** 19 20

21 22 23 24 25 26 27 28 29 **30**   27+3=**30**

Words to Know

burrow—an underground home for animals.

groom—to clean and make a neat appearance.

perch—to sit on top of something.

prairie—flat land covered in tall grasses.

Web Sites

To learn more about counting by 3s, visit ABDO Publishing Company on the World Wide Web at **www.abdopublishing.com.** Web sites about counting are featured on our Book Links page. These links are routinely monitored and updated to provide the most current information available.

1 2 **3** 4 5 **6** 7 8 **9** 10 11 **12** 13 14 **15** 16 17
18 19 20 **21** 22 23 **24** 25 26 **27** 28 29 **30**